The Yorkie Who Sings at Midnight

Janne Swearengen
Illustrated by Kalyb James

To Rebecca with
many thanks!

Janne

First Printing, 2021

ISBN 978-1-938819-89-6

Printed in the United States of America

115 Metroplex Blvd
Pearl, MS 39208

www.agpearl.com

Dedication

This book is dedicated to Dr. Sylvia Stewart who was a champion for treating rescued and shelter animals at Monroe Street Animal Clinic in Jackson, Mississippi. Godspeed Doc Sylvia... you have a legion of friends waiting for you at the Rainbow Bridge, including your beloved Boston Terrier, Monroe.

You also have a legion of human friends who knew, felt, and deeply appreciated your passion for the 'least of these'. You left too soon because somewhere there is a need for you.

A portion of the proceeds from the sale of this book goes to the Animal Rescue Fund of Mississippi. ARF/Mississippi was established by Elizabeth Jackson in 2005 following the devastating impact of Hurricane Katrina on the thousands of displaced, injured, and abandoned animals along the Gulf Coast of Mississippi. A 501(c)(3) no-kill' shelter, ARF/Mississippi remains committed to the belief that all animals deserve a chance at a meaningful and loving home.

Animal Rescue Fund
Of Mississippi

(https://www.arfms.org/)

Acknowledgments

To Larry Swearengen, affectionately known nation-wide as Big Solid, the husband who wanted a Yorkie. His absolute loving soul for all the dogs we have rescued, lost, rescued, lost, and rescued again seals him in my heart as the best decision I have ever made.

To Kalyb James, a young man with a huge talent. Not only did he absolutely nail the look we wanted for our illustrations, but he also did it immediately. The very FIRST TIME. And we were off and running! Kalyb is a straight A high school student who is no doubt going to make a name for himself in the future. We are more than delighted and excited to introduce him to the world.

To Karen Clark, who first read this as a small essay-ish post on Facebook and suggested it become a book. We had never given it a thought, but the idea stuck and struck such a clear note, we could not let it go. And once we found Kalyb, well, the rest is history, Thank you, Karen. We hope you are pleased.

And to Susan Marquez, President of the Mississippi Writers Guild, believer in the written word and deliverer of said written word in countless magazines, books, essays, and articles. Susan took us under her writing wing to believe, edit, challenge, and insist that we could possibly make a difference with Angela's story. We will forever and always be in your debt.

"It is only with the heart that one sees rightly; what is essential is invisible to the eye."

Antoine de Saint-Exupery

PART ONE
IN MY OWN WORDS

CHAPTER ONE
MY EARLY LIFE

I do not recollect much of my puppyhood other than trying to drink as much of Mama's milk as I could. I think I was the smallest of my brothers and sisters because they always squeezed me out of the way. The same thing happened when I started eating real food. We would all crowd around one dish and bury our noses in our food. I remained the smallest one of all because there was not enough food to go around, and I would get crowded out by my brothers and sisters.

IT seemed like we were always hunting for something to eat. We never got petted or held; we just stayed in a cage with our Mama. Then one day, the cage door opened, and Mama was carried out. We never saw her again, but we could hear her crying for us. But I did not let that get in the way of being a busy girl. I wanted to learn about 'stuffs', and I spent most of my awake time just looking all around my cage. I played with my siblings a lot; we would growl and bark and chase each other around. Sometimes we would play so hard we'd tump over and wind up in a big heap of little bitty puppies. We would all pile on top of each other at night to sleep and to stay warm. Some of us would snore, but some would cry because they were hungry, and one of my brothers would growl. It was then I discovered that I could make a different sound - a musical sound. I could sing!

BEFORE long there were not as many of us. My sisters and brothers were taken away one-by-one until there was just me. And then the Boss-Lady picked me up and put me in the hands of a stranger. "Here," she said. "Take her. She's the runt of the litter. She don't even weigh a pound. You can have her for just $300. She'll make tiny Yorkie puppies that you can sell easy and get a good price." It was the end of my baby days; it was the first time I heard that I was called a Yorkie. It was also the introduction to a world of struggle.

CHAPTER TWO
THE SUFFERIN' YEARS

FOR the next many years, I lived in a place that was jam-packed with other dogs. Mostly smaller dogs like me and there were lots and lots of them. We never went outside so we relieved ourselves wherever and whenever we had to. I had puppies every year, and sometimes twice a year. As soon as they could eat a little puppy food, I was taken away from them. Then they would be gone, and I would be made ready to have more.

AS the years went by, more and more dogs came to this house. We were almost living on top of each other. Some of us began to get sick. Fleas were everywhere. They were all over our skin, in our ears, everywhere. We scratched so much we had sores. We also got sores from mats that would form in our fur, especially long-haired dogs like me. The mats would get so bad, the skin underneath would become infected and raw. Once a week, we would get hosed down to rinse off all the filth and waste. We would shake and shiver for a long time after, especially in the wintertime. It got COLD!!

THERE was never enough to eat and what we did get did not taste very good and was not very healthy. I kept having puppies until my body did not work as well as it once did. In fact, I started losing my teeth when I was still young. Pretty soon, all of them were gone and I had to use the gums in my lower jaw to get food out of the dish or off the floor. As time went on by, the bone in my jaw just melted away. When that happened, I could not keep my tongue in my mouth. It was difficult to eat food that was hard, but I did the best I could.

AFTER a few more years, I started having trouble making babies, so I was taken out of my birthin' cage home where I raised my babies and left to roam the house with dozens of other dogs. We were always sick. We got eye infections all the time that hurt really bad, and we were always rubbing our eyes on the dirty floor or each other. Some of my house-mates could not see anymore, so they were always running into the wall or falling downstairs. Us 'wimmen' began to get larger and larger breasts from feeding so many puppies that even though we did not have puppies anymore, we still had all kinds of bumps and lumps there. I still have them all over my little belly.

ABOUT that time, I got a 'crackerjack' on one of my eyes and it got so bad, I could not see out of it anymore. But at least I could see out of the other one - not very well, but enough to get out of the way of other dogs milling around. I was deaf in one ear, so it was hard for me to figure out where noises were coming from. And then, almost all of us got re-ally sick with worms that got in our hearts. We had no idea what was wrong with us, only that we could not breathe good or catch our breaths. Some of us even died. These worms are just awful since they grow and grow and have little worms in the heart until the heart cannot function at all.

THESE were hard years...I never got petted or talked to sweet. Every day and night were the same, the stench of in-fection, the taste of stale molded food, the sounds of misery, and the constant itch from fleas. There was no kindness in the Hoarding House.

I lived there for a really long time and to help me pass the sufferin' times, I turned to singing during the night. Singing made me feel safe and happy, like I was special. Nobody really paid attention to my singin' because they were crying or barking or squealing or whining or havin' babies. Then one day, some people found out about the Hoarding House. They picked us up and took us to a shelter named The Animal Rescue Fund of Mississippi. Even though I was really scared, I sang my way through the fear of 'new' and things took a turn for the better.

CHAPTER 3
THE KINDNESS YEARS

AS soon as we were accepted into the shelter, we were all taken to doctors. Since there were so many of us with so many issues that needed attention, more than one veterinarian was called on to check us out. We all got a good goin' over with our medical needs addressed as quickly as possible.

I remember the first time I went outside and my feet touched grass. It scared me so bad I was afraid to walk any more. I just got stuck in place. The grass was a very strange feeling under my paws, scratchy and soft at the same time. I had to be picked up and moved from place to place. What I wanted to do was run inside and hide.

THEN we were parceled out to some nice people called Foster People who would help find us homes. Me and some of my friends went to a Nice Lady who gave us warm beds, great food, sweet words, and lots of attention; she told us every night that she would help us find us a forever family. The Nice Lady called me Thumbelina because I am a tiny little thing. Most people want young dogs that are healthy and will live a long time. Most folks don't want an older dog, especially one like me — a twelve-year-old, heartworm positive, toothless, eating challenged, hard of hearing, teeny Yorkie with a 'crackerjack' in her eye.

THE first thing was to get me as healthy as possible and that's where Nice Lady put me on the road to kindness and well-being. She made sure I started getting treatment for the worms in my heart. The first shot made me feel really sick, but I kept right on singin' because it made me feel better. After that first shot, I also got 'spaded' so there would for sure be no more babies and that sure made me sing!

AND then....and then...one day, the Nice Lady told me that I was bein' adopted, whatever that meant! It kinda scared me when she wrapped me up in a little blanket and carried me to the car. I sang a bit, but I couldn't stay on pitch...my nerves were so rattled. She took me out of the car and put me in the arms of my New Mama. I was shakin' like a leaf; I was so scared. We got in another car and drove away. I kept shakin' and couldn't carry a tune in a bucket. I got lots of pets and sweet words from these new people while we drove away from my sisters and Nice Lady.

WHEN I got to my new house, I ran all over the place. I wanted to go out; I kept jumping up on the door. I couldn't be still. I was terrified. My new brother sniffed me once and got back under his blanket. I finally noticed that there were several comfy beds that I could get in and relax. But I couldn't sing...my voice was lost.

THAT was a while back...now I'm all settled in. I have a special bowl to help me eat because of my melted bottom jaw. I have three beds with blankets in each one. I get delicious food twice a day and treats when I go outside to go pots. You should see how I run like the wind to my special bowl of food and treats! And I am now called Angela because my new folks think I am an angel but I like both my names Angela and Thumbelina!"

I get to sleep in the sunshine as it passes through the back door; and I have 'power rugs' all over the floor to keep me from slipping. I get walked outside twice a day and get to smell all kinds of new things. Grass under my paws doesn't bother me a bit anymore! Now, after midnight, I practice my scales to keep on singin'.

I am most particular about my hair...I like it all fluffed out and spikey, so I spend a lot of time rubbing my head on the blanket to get just the right look or shaking my head really good, so my hairs stick straight out.

I love to 'high-five' when someone wishes to pet me; it sure didn't take long for me to love being petted; but it did take some time for me to get comfortable resting in my Mama's lap.

Each night, when my Mama goes to bed, I fly into the bedroom and jump in my most favorite bed, get a night-time pet, then tuck myself in. Around midnight, I feel the song of hope and love rise in my throat...and I sing Because I'm Happy. I am Angela Thumbelina. I am the Yorkie Who Sings at Midnight.

CHAPTER 4
MAY I SPEAK? - ANGELA'S BROTHER

I have my two cents worth to add to the Kindness Years. I am called Mike Tyson and I am a badass Chihuahua. I was found on the street hairless and almost at Death's door. After some hard work and lots of medicine and love, I recovered and needed a home. Being a tiny boy, one would have thought I would be adopted right off the bat. That wasn't the case because I growled and tried to bite folks. I stayed in the office at the Animal Rescue Fund of Mississippi' for months, sleepin' under a desk without anyone to give me a home.

THEN one day I was gathered up and brought "out front" to meet two peoples. They held me, they asked questions, they cried a little, and, you know what, they took me home. That's right – HOME! That was over a year ago and I can truthfully say I won the adopt-a-dog lottery. We have had our ups and downs because I have some issues with anger management. When I first got here, I had a nice little inside house that I stayed in all the time. I slept under a blanket in the day; when my Mama tried to get me out to go pots, I snarled, snapped, and even bit her.

EVERY day around 5:30 in the afternoon (quittin' time for most working folks), I still get really really angry at my Daddy. I snap at him and try to bite. But if he claps his hands and calls me to his lap, I run like the wind. I love lap time. I growl when he picks me up, but when he puts me next to him, life is the best ever. Something bad happened to me a long time ago that makes me very anxious/angry around that time of day. I can't even remember it exactly, and maybe that's a good thing.

I'M sharing this because even though I have some behaviors that may be a challenge, I'm still a really good boy and want to keep my forever home. And that brings me to my 'sister' Angela. I was not a happy camper when Mama and Daddy walked in with her. I liked being an only chihuahua. I liked getting all the attention. But she seemed harmless and didn't smell bad. She didn't try to eat my food or get in my bed. At night, I snuggle up to my Mama and my new sister curls up in her bed on the floor and sleeps like a little baby. Well, until she starts to sing. So, what's the point in being jealous of a little girl who sings? We both have what we always wanted and that's an always place to be.

PART TWO

CHAPTER 5
ANGELA'S PARENTS SPEAK

THERE was not a question in our minds when we saw a picture of Angela from Dr. Sylvia Stewart's clinic; we knew she would be ours. We decided some time back to focus on adopting the elders and/or hospice dogs so they may live out the rest of their days in a loving home. Even with all of her issues of heartworms (for which she has now been successfully treated), the 'crackerjack' in her right eye and the one growing in her left, the mammary gland tumors which are a continuing concern, and her advanced age, she was destined to be ours for however long she had. We settled in for taking care of an 'invalid' Yorkie.

WELL, she came to us full of life, or as we say, "a going concern." It's hard for us to believe she is an elder lady and were it not for some of the physical indications (hearing loss, her 'crackerjacks', the loss of her teeth and significant loss of bone in her lower jaw), we'd think her more middle aged. She tries to play with her brother, Mike Tyson, but he cannot be bothered. Angela quickly became as much a part of our lives as the air we breathe. We are constantly amused at how she likes – no, demands – to spike her hair out like Phyllis Diller. We love the little noises she makes when she eats from her special bowl, her passionate barks as she waits at the back door for her Mama to come home, and her multiple patrol trips around the house during the day. Yet, the mystery of her nighttime singing is perhaps the singular characteristic that sets her apart from any animal we have ever had. It's just too bad you can't hear her from a book. She has a little Yorkie-sized donut bed she adores, and she can be heard tuning up anytime from midnight to four in the morning.

WE simply adore her. And we know our hearts will be shattered when her time is up; yet it's because of her and so many who are forgotten or ignored, we'll do it again and again until we find ourselves incapable of functioning on our own and need someone to adopt us.

CHAPTER 6
THE POWER OF FOSTERING

Note: For the sake of brevity, we single out dogs - male and female - in the following chapters dealing with fostering, adoption, and special needs adoptions. However, please understand that foster care and adoption covers the entirety of the animal kingdom, seriously.

ONE of the most important functions for a rescue organization is that of foster placement. Amazing volunteers and volunteer families open their homes and hearts to animals and provide care in a home environment while assisting the shelter staff with finding a suitable and loving "forever home." The shelter typically covers the medical expenses that are incurred to assure the 'adoptability' of an animal', while the foster family provides the love and security necessary to bring their charge to full and adoptable health.

ACCORDING to the Mississippi Animal Rescue Fund's website, providing foster care has three primary functions:
- Foster homes increase the chances of a successful match and decreases the potential for an animal being returned.

- Fostering teaches us more about the personality of the pets. Just like people, dogs have different personalities and needs. For example, a large young dog is not a good match for apartment living. The foster parent can advise the potential adopting family of those needs and guide them to a more suitable match. Likewise, an older potential adoptive family might be much more comfortable with an older, less active dog that can be happy as a clam in lap, has good manners, and is well-house trained. Fostering 'parents can watch the interaction between a potential adopting family during a supervised visit to assess the behaviors exhibited by both parties, namely the dog and the potential adoptive family.

• Fostering frees space at the shelter for another rescue animal. As much as all shelters would love to say, 'we have room for more', they rarely do. And, frankly, for extra small dogs typically under ten pounds, the activity and noise levels in a moderate to large shelter are extremely stressful. If these aren't reasons enough, we'd like to add a fourth one:

• Fostering provides personalized attention to animals who need an elevated level of care. Many rescued animals, in fact, most rescued animals, arrive with medical and/or psychological issues that warrant attention before a permanent adoptive home is found. If medical care is provided and an animal needs a period of after care or rehabilitation, placement with a qualified and approved foster home provides a much better healing environment than the actual shelter. The same holds true for animals who have experienced emotional trauma. Foster care offers the animal a safe place to recover from surgery, injury, or abuse. Most shelters have strict requirements regarding the health (physical and emotional) of a rescued animal prior to a permanent adoption. Examples include assuring that the animal recovers from being spayed or neutered; treating the animal for heartworms; and supporting the rehabilitation of an animal which has been injured. Foster providers are adept at changing bandages, giving medications, providing treatments (such as skin issues) in an atmosphere of kindness and emotional support.

WITH our tongue securely fastened in our cheek, we submit that Foster people fall into two major categories...the Continuing Foster and the Failed Foster.

THE Continuing Foster is the person or family who will take in a dog or even litter of puppies, provide all the love, care, and attention they need with the sole purpose of finding them the best home possible. These dogs are loved, provided guidance with house-breaking, walking on a lead, simple good manners — all the things that make a dog a pleasure to be adopted. When a good match is found, the Continuing Foster celebrates yet another forever home is found and sends both dog and new family happily on their way. Almost simultaneously, the Continuing Foster reaches for the phone, calls the local shelter, and asks if there is a dog in need of fostering. For them, fostering is their significant place along the path of finding a forever home for a 'shelter dog'.

THE Failed Foster does essentially the same thing. The major difference is that when the shelter staff calls to tell the Foster that a someone or a family is interested in the dog they are fostering, the Foster's heart clenches, blood pressure increases, tear ducts begin to overflow, and the final decision is made. "I love this dog so much. I just can't give this dog up. I will keep this dog." And, once again, the attempt to place this dog in a forever home has, well, failed. We belong in that category.

CHAPTER 7
WHY WE ADOPT

WHY do we choose to adopt from a shelter? For as long as we can remember, animals have been our best pals, great listeners, givers of unconditional love, and companions par excellénce. Dogs love us for who we are, not how we appear; they love us when we cry, or even when we are angry. There does not exist a human emotion they do not also feel and/ or sense. They miss us when we are gone and greet us with ebullient joy when we return. They do not care what color we are or if we have physical and/or emotional problems. We have learned how to deal with the pain of losing them, the grief that is felt in every molecule we have, and then making the decision to, yes, do it all again. One more journey, one more opening the heart, one more dog.

DOGS do not voluntarily become shelter dogs and there-fore tend come to the shelter with emotional or behavior-al baggage (or both) for which they did not ask. Maybe they were an impulse buy in a parking lot or roadside who turned out to be too much work to housebreak, train, or even feed; or a dog that spent most of his or her life on a chain with lit-tle shelter and has no understanding of walking on a lead or having a comfortable place to sleep; or an abandoned "pet" left behind when the family moved; or an abused and beat-en down dog; or a dog left at the mercy of the streets and illnesses; or possibly bait dogs for illegal dog fighting operations to name a few. And then there are the elder dogs, the ones whose people no longer care for them, or for whom there is no longer time to address or attend to the issues that come with an aging pet.

MANY folks want to know why we choose to adopt dogs nearing the end of their lives. As one who spent the better part of my working life in long term care facilities, I have always been attracted to the elderly and their storied lives.

THERE is no better description of the loss that aging brings than the magnificent John Prine song Hello in There. Youth gives way to adulthood, busy with parenting and providing for our families; adulthood seems to 'evaporate' with the infirmities of growing older. The senses that were once sharp, are now dulled. The creative mind loses traction and wanders from one idea to another without a focal point. The muscular body can no longer sustain the activities of youth. And try as we may, everything slows down. Freedoms once taken for granted are lost and the independence we cherished disappears in increments. Catastrophic or terminal illnesses take center stage as life slowly comes to an end, or at least a transition point.

AS humans, we understand, though may not like, or enjoy, the aging dilemma and the inevitability of those gradual or sudden losses. Yet, animals often find themselves part of a family one day and the alone in a shelter the next. For whatever reason, they are no longer in their home, they are in a system. They are no longer capable of producing puppies to sell on the side of the road or in a parking lot, so they are dropped off at a shelter or, even worse, left at a roadside. They are simply too much trouble, too expensive to care for, or both, due to incontinence and medical needs, so they are dropped off at a local shelter.

THE enormous number of elder animals in shelters stands as a sad commentary on how we treat "the least of these." So, this is where our hearts are. To us, there is nothing more distressing than to hear or learn of an aged pet who has been surrendered to a shelter because they are ill, frail, or sadly, to make room for a new puppy. This is our mission, and you'd be wrong if you thought it all sadness and pain. We have the most rewarding task of providing a loving home for an elder states-dog. We provide a lap in which to rest. We provide food that is easy on an edentulous mouth, sensitive digestive system, or specially formulated to meet special needs. And we provide medical care to ease pain and address illnesses. It is not a path for everyone, but it is our path. Sometimes folks are surprised by the joy an older dog can bring. Such is the case with Angela.

THERE are times, however, when even the best intended adoptions do not work out, no matter how hard the adoptive family has tried to make it so. Unforeseen circumstances often intervene and wreak havoc on a family's life; catastrophic illness, change in household dynamic such as a divorce, loss of spouse or - God forbid - a child, unanticipated employment status, just to name a few. And, despite every alternative imagined to maintain an intact adoption and family, change must be made. Reputable shelters and non-brick-and-mortar rescue confederations have a clause in their adoption contracts that requires the adopted animal be returned to the shelter and not re-homed outside of the shelter purview. In the event of a long distance need to surrender, consideration should be made by contacting the adoptive shelter to discuss more locally oriented options.

CHAPTER 8
ADOPTING A SPECIAL NEEDS ANIMAL

NOT all rescue animals are perfect physical specimens, yet many have the capability of living many more years of a happy and healthy life. Elderly or aged animals are especially vulnerable to becoming shelter animals, often surrendered after developing issues of aging such as arthritis, incontinence, dementia, or loss of sensory functions (vision or hearing). Animals which have been maimed due to trauma, disease, or amputation are also very difficult to place. And finally, animals with challenging behaviors are among the most complicated of placements and the adoption of such an animal should be weighed very carefully. Often dogs with behavioral issues will wind up being adopted by the person(s) fostering them. We can testify to that with a previous 'failed foster' named Marley, The Wayward Poodle

Marley, The Wayward Poodle
Marley gave us a run for our money from the day we said we want to foster him until the day he went across that Rainbow Bridge to become healthy and troubled no more. In fact, we even returned him to the Animal Rescue Fund of Mississippi due to his volatile and aggressive nature. But, as we stood in ARF's front office, crying our eyes out, we decided to try one more time. We could NOT let him return to an environment that would exacerbate his issues of hyper-anxiety and hypersensitivity. Six years later, we stood in Doc Sylvia's clinic, once again crying our eyes out, cradling him, as she allowed him to become whole again on the Other Side of The Rainbow Bridge

CHAPTER 9
READY, SET, GO!

SINCE you are reading this (and hopefully enjoying it), your heart and conscience may be leading you to take some kind of action. It's now a matter of what that action can be. Let's explore that.

IF you are on the 'maybe/maybe not' fence, consider searching for websites or social media pages to identify local shelters. Chances are, you will notice the intense need for help both financially and hands on. Becoming a volunteer is always a good way to learn how the shelter functions and how you can best be part of a team. Shelters almost always love to have folks who will walk and exercise the dogs. Sometimes dogs who are frightened by placement in a shelter may be soothed by someone who will sit with the dog and simply read to it. If your interest is in other animals such as cats, rabbits (or any member of the animal kingdom), it is best to check with the shelter for in-depth information and specific needs volunteer may help address.

WHETHER you find yourself leaning towards providing foster care or in adopting, contact the shelter and learn what their foster care and adoption process entails and what they expect from you. Shelters nationwide are full to the brim with dogs and other animals which have been surrendered, neglected, abused, over-bred, or otherwise felt to no longer be of worth or use. Visit and see for yourself. Most shelters have an application process to assure the best outcomes for the animal and the foster or adoptee.

IF you have never been to a shelter before, a word of caution. You will most likely find it overwhelming. Initially by the noise of many barking dogs, then by the sheer numbers of animals housed and cared for, and then by your own heart's struggle to take it all in. After your visit, go home and sift through your thoughts, feelings, reactions, and emotions. Whatever you decide, know that if your journey stops here, you gave it your best and the demands are too high. Figure out a way to help that doesn't require your personal involvement — donate.

IF you choose to move forward, step into a world that will reward you ten times over by either fostering or adopting a dog in need. You are a changed human.

PART THREE
FULL CIRCLE

CHAPTER 10
PARTING WORDS FROM ANGELA
To Love Somebody Forward

FIRST, thank you for reading and heeding my little book. It has been a great joy for me to share my story with you, especially because it has a happy ending. I have learned to make the best of my life, even though there were some awful times when I wanted to lash out, to be angry, to snap and snarl. But somehow, I resolved to be sweet, funny, inquisitive, and loving. And that has kept me strong and kept me singing. It is what I call "loving someone forward." And now, my wish is to love you forward as I have learned to do; to teach you the power to meet the bad things in life in the spirit of reconciliation rather than rancor; with a paw up rather than a punch down. There can be no love without joy, so why not choose joy?

I sure did, and I would not change anything that got me where I am today. Now, excuse me while I go find my Mama's lap and we watch some TV. Bye Bye.

Made in the USA
Middletown, DE
20 June 2021

42760747R10024